TEN
FEET
TALL

Step Into Your Truth and
Change Your Freaking World

BRANDON FARBSTEIN

This book is a memoir. It reflects the author's present recollections of experiences over time and how he has used those experiences to change his life. Some names and characteristics have been changed, some events have been compressed, and some dialogue has been recreated.

Interior design by IDA FIA SVENINGSSON
Cover design by IDA FIA SVENINGSSON

Print ISBN: 13: 978-1-7328002-1-2

DEDICATION

This book is dedicated to you.
Always remember to stay true to
yourself and you will soar.

All my gratitude to everyone who
has supported my journey. I'm so thankful
for the neverending strength and
love you give me.

To my Mom, Dad, and sister Brooke:
I am who I am because of you. Thank you for
always showing me what I am capable of.

CONTENTS

A LIFETIME OF CHANGE

Nearly 2,000 sets of eyes watched me, waiting for my mouth to open. Fifteen years of simply existing in the world had led me to this singular moment on stage at Carpenter Theatre in my hometown of Richmond, Virginia, a moment that would allow me to finally feel worthy of living. For the first time, I decided that my strength and power would reveal itself through genuine and wholehearted vulnerability.

The stage had been my most cherished environment since the age of eight, when my parents signed me up for theater classes with a local nonprofit. From the beginning, I loved being in front of an audience, making them smile and laugh, and helping them escape their reality. I knew that I was adding something — however small — to their day. Yet, in my performances I was always a character. I always portrayed someone else. This time it was different. I was speaking to a sold-out crowd for TEDxRVA. My talk, which I called *Upwardly Mobile*, was the story of how I dealt with my doctor's suggestion to get a conventional mobility device when I was in my early teens, and my decision to break from his advice and innovate my own solution. The talk was the first time I would be onstage as myself — as Brandon Farbstein — and not as a character. I would be baring my soul as I shared my story. And I didn't know what to expect.

At age two, I was diagnosed with metatropic dysplasia, a form of dwarfism so rare that fewer than one hundred cases have ever been reported in medical history. Over the years, the daily challenge of living in a world where most everyone looked down on me created a constant self-induced state of limitation. My degenerative skeletal condition and short stature used to hold me back from nearly everything. As my world grew before me, I became keenly aware of how people interacted with each other and how invisible I felt in comparison.

Giving the TEDx talk finally allowed me to own my story. It was about embracing it, extracting the lessons, and transforming it into fuel to propel me forward. After fifteen years of merely existing and letting my suffering lead, I put my trust in the thousands of strangers sitting in front of me. My six minutes on the iconic red circular rug would turn into a complete rewiring of my life. Things would be different. I would finally stop being the victim and start being the victor.

It is not a stretch to say that through my TEDx talk I learned to effectively deal with my pain and transform my life. I realized that the road to fulfillment is achieved through human connection and living your purpose and passion each day.

Since then, I have continued to speak up and have reached over two million individuals across the globe, both virtually and in person. My mission every day is to change the world's perception, one perspective at a time. I want people to embrace their own story and not get stuck in their own struggles.

Rather than avoiding or covering up pain, it is utterly life-changing to recognize how universal pain and suffering truly is. While we cannot control the pain we encounter, we can manage our reaction and create ways around it. Focusing on what we have rather than craving what we lack ensures growth, even when one's physical being prevents it.

My upwardly mobile journey began with six impactful minutes on stage three years ago. I decided that my diagnosis is not who I am and realized we are only defined by what we allow ourselves to be. Since then, I have discovered my unique power and have made it my mission to become one of the world's most impactful motivational speakers. I have seen people react and transform when they connect with my story. In September 2017, I became the youngest member of the National Speakers Association. I have given talks to audiences ranging from homeless individuals and underprivileged youth to Fortune 500 companies to conferences of thousands. My work has brought me alongside moguls such as Tony Robbins, Lewis Howes, Gary Vaynerchuk, and many other wildly successful entrepreneurs and A-List celebrities. I share my journey with each audience, and no matter the background, age, or life circumstance of the attendees, **I find the beauty in human connection.**

I am most grateful when audience members open up to me and share their own story. These are the moments I cherish, as we both walk away with hope and optimism. It is amazing to enter a room full of strangers and walk out with the feeling of universal love and a full shift in perspective. It is fascinating to see the beauty in all circumstances when you approach life with a lens of compassion and empathy.

Regardless of where you are in life, my goal for this book is that it may fuel you on your journey. I hope it will aid you as you shift your mindset and continue to evolve. I hope it will fill you with a sense of empowerment and help you tap into the tools you already have, the ones that will enable you to achieve the life you are meant to live. Perhaps it will help you discover new ways to tackle the challenges of life. Most of all, may this book remind you that no matter what you've been through or what you're going to go through, **you are absolutely unstoppable.**

THE POWER OF ONE

LIFE HAPPENS FOR US,

NOT TO US.

– TONY ROBBINS

CHAPTER 1

ONE THING CAN CHANGE EVERYTHING

It is fair to say that giving my TEDx talk changed my life. It was a catalyst that set so many other changes into motion. But here is the radical thing: If not for a chance encounter in an airport, it may never have happened.

In October 2014 my family and I were waiting to catch a flight out of our hometown Richmond, bound for Miami to visit my great-grandmother. I had my yellow "Segway-like" mobility device with me, and, as usual, it piqued the curiosity of those around us. Picture, basically, a cross between a Lamborghini and a Transformer. I know. A pretty epic combination. As we were in line for security a woman came up to me and started making small talk. Our conversation was pleasant, though I didn't think too much about it. As we walked toward the gate, we kept our conversation going and things started to get interesting.

I learned that this talkative traveller named Heather was one of the first organizers of TEDx events and a top TEDx coach. She had been passing through Richmond, and just so happened to end up on our flight. I told her my story and we exchanged contact information. Seven months later, I was on stage as a TEDx speaker. Granted, it was a rigorous vetting process, but the opportunity would not have presented itself at that time had I not been open to exchange meaningful dialogue with this stranger.

One singular moment, *one* chance encounter, *one* opportunity seized upon changed everything. That's the power of one.

What I love about the power of one is that it means we do not have to tackle everything all at once in order to see real change in our lives. Trying to attack every aspect of our lives at the same time is simply too overwhelming. It is a recipe for confusion, burnout, and disappointment. The power of one means that we can affect huge transformation in our lives just by taking the next step forward. In other words, **we don't have to change everything for everything to change**.

Take a minute to think back on your own greatest accomplishments, your personal defining moments. How many of them started out small? How many of them were tiny, seemingly accidental occurrences that led to something much bigger? I would bet it is more prevalent than you think. Consider what that means for your life in this moment: Right now, there are any number of first steps you can take to transform your life, to advance to that next place. You don't have to worry about mapping out the entire plan. Focus on step one, and take action.

Maybe the process will feel inconsequential at first. That's okay. That won't stop you from getting

ONE SINGULAR MOMENT,

ONE CHANCE ENCOUNTER,

ONE OPPORTUNITY SEIZED UPON

CHANGED EVERYTHING.

THAT'S THE POWER OF ONE.

where you want to go. Starting on your path and being committed is one of the best ways to bring the power of one into full effect in your life. The things that we want — whether a job opportunity, a relationship, or a particular experience — have a way of finding us when we're ready and open to them.

If I had met Heather six months or a year earlier, I really don't know if it would have had the same result. Our encounter happened at the exact moment I was most ready and willing to take advantage of it. This is something certain people might tie in with religion — some attribute it to Divine Intervention. If that sentiment resonates with you, great. But I don't think you need to be religious to see this principle in action in your life. It's simple: success attracts success. Positivity attracts positivity. The universe has our back. The people around you want to succeed, and they want you to succeed. There is tremendous power in that.

Maybe the person sitting next to you at the airport gate doesn't hold the key to your next personal or professional breakthrough (or maybe he or she does). The point is not to single out the ultimate next opportunity, but to realize that there is always another opportunity out there, and one after that. Life is full of amazing possibilities to move forward. The question is, are you going to take advantage of them?

CHAPTER 2

DO ONE THING

If one thing can change everything, then each day presents a genuine opportunity to transform our lives. Every day is *our* day, *our* time, *our* moment. In order to take advantage of that, we need to not only have the mindset that one thing can change everything, but we need to put that truth into action. After all, actions, not just thoughts, create progress.

Here is the challenge I want to present to you: **Each day, do one thing to impact your life or the life of someone around you.** Just one thing. That's all it takes.

The thing you pick could be in your job or school, it could be in your personal life, or in your creative life. It could be big: making that phone call to mend a relationship with a lost friend. Or it could be small: striking up a conversation with someone in your office or at school who you've noticed seems lonely. It could be one thing you do for yourself or one thing you do for someone else. The point isn't necessarily what today's one thing will be. It is that you are committed to taking positive action every single day, no matter what.

The reason this works is simple: momentum. We all have it, or we would not be living. When we get in the habit of asking ourselves every day, "What are we going to do to move forward in a positive direction?," we take control of the natural momentum of our lives and point it toward the things we want. Small changes compound, and day by day the way becomes clearer.

The "Do One Thing" mentality has become a core philosophy for me. It is no longer something I have to think about in order to practice. But if it is a new concept for you, you can try framing it as a question you use to start your day: "What am I going to accomplish today? What am I going to do to contribute to my life and to the lives of others?"

REMEMBER,

YOU DON'T HAVE TO

CHANGE EVERYTHING

FOR EVERYTHING

TO CHANGE.

And after some time, these thoughts will become part of your natural mindset.

Maybe you want to write a question down on a slip of paper and tack it by your bed so that it is the first thing you see when you wake up in the morning. Or maybe you want to repeat it like a mantra as you get ready for work or for school. We all have many tools at our disposal for making changes. The key is repetition. Doing one thing only works if it is a lifestyle, if it's a given. It is ineffective if it is something you just do every now and then. Again, we are talking about building positive momentum— rewiring how our brains see the day and then putting that new brainpower into action.

So, what if this all sounds great, but you are unclear about where to begin?

My suggestion would be to look at what is already happening in your day. What environments are you in? Who are you around? Each one of us has the ability to add value to the lives of others, whether we are a student, employee, friend, or neighbor. Think about what you can do to contribute to someone's day, however large or small the action is. Regardless of what is going on in your day, I guarantee you will come into contact with someone who could benefit from a smile or a word of encouragement. There is no better way to enhance our own lives than to make someone else's day a little bit better.

When in doubt, keep it simple. Remember, *you don't have to change everything for everything to change.*

Our lives are filled with opportunities to make the world better, and in turn give us the ultimate sense of fulfillment. When we make a point of paying attention to and acting on these possibilities, we set ourselves up for massive success. Start today. Ask yourself what your next thing will be, and then *do it.*

CHAPTER 3

NO REASON
TO SUFFER

Every day we make choices about how we want to live our lives. We cannot prevent negative things from happening to us, but we can choose how we react. We can decide whether they will stop us in our tracks or become the motivation that propels us toward success.

The moment I made the decision to leave my high school, I solidified this principle in my own life. Not the traditional path toward advancement, right? But, it ended up being my road to incredible learning opportunities.

The same year I got my "Segway" mobility device, I also started my freshman year at one of the best public schools in Virginia. It was the "whole package": amazing sports teams, great classes, and remarkable test scores. But almost right away, I became the center of vicious cyberbullying attacks from students there.

During my first week of classes I became aware of a Tweet circulating on social media. It was written by a student at a neighboring high school. "If somebody gets me a picture of the midget on the Segway, I'll pay you $5," it said. I kind of knew that I was in for a rough time starting high school. But even still, I was shocked by how quickly the attacks started and how cruel they were. From there, things escalated. I was tormented daily in person and online about my size, about my mobility device, even about being Jewish.

I felt stranded and completely isolated. I could see nobody, and nobody could see me. Maybe you have felt this way, too. You do not need to be in high school to feel like an outsider or as if you don't belong with the people around you.

It wasn't all bad news: The bullying became the inspiration for my TEDx talk. Without having had that experience, my encounter with Heather and our subsequent conversation may have never led me to my purposeful path. By the start of my junior year, I was exhausted and demoralized. The toll of the cyberbullying was impacting every aspect of my life: my grades were suffering, relationships became nonexistent, and my stress was at an all time high. For the first time since I was eleven, I had thoughts of ending my life to make the suffering stop.

My breaking point — which actually became my turning point — happened just before Thanksgiving of my junior year. During the holiday break, a picture appeared on an Instagram account. It was a distorted photograph of me giving my TEDx talk. Underneath, the caption read: "Midget performs for Auschwitz concentration camp before going to gas chambers." Other posts and comments were equally horrifying. This was one of many cruel and derogatory photos and commentary, including video of me on my mobility device in my high school hallway.

WE CANNOT PREVENT NEGATIVE THINGS

FROM HAPPENING TO US,

BUT WE CAN CHOOSE HOW WE REACT.

WE CAN DECIDE WHETHER THEY

WILL STOP US IN OUR TRACKS

OR BECOME THE MOTIVATION

THAT PROPELS US TOWARD SUCCESS.

I knew as soon as I saw those posts that I had had enough. I needed to be rid of the toxic environment I was in once and for all. The Monday after Thanksgiving break, I went to my parents and told them that school day would be my last. I didn't care if I had to drop out or get my GED. I was not going to languish in that debilitating circumstance any longer.

That morning I went into the administrator's office and told her that I wanted to finish my junior year online. It took a lot of negotiation to make it happen, but eventually we made the necessary arrangements. I finished out that school year online, and then started on my senior year at a community college. I said goodbye to the toxicity once and for all. Since then, I am grateful to have completed my course work for my high school diploma and have been accepted into university.

Pain is universal to human existence. We can't choose to have bad things not happen to us. What we *can choose* is our response. We do not have to stay in situations that hurt us. We do not have to settle for cruel relationships and harmful environments.

We consistently underestimate how much we can alter our lives and how powerful those changes can be. A decision to say "no more" to what is hurting us is not just about clearing our lives of useless suffering. It is also about opening up space for things that bring the good into our journey.

When I made the decision to finish out my high school education online, I not only freed myself of what could have been a lethal environment but also set myself up to go further along the path toward my purpose. Online classes meant I had more time on my hands during the conventional school day, as I typically did my work in the evenings. I began filling my days by networking and booking more speaking engagements. My speaking career grew faster than I could have ever imagined because of one change: ridding my life of something that was harming me.

Where have you gotten stuck in situations and environments that aren't serving you? What are you missing out on because suffering is preventing you from living your greatest life? It may not be a physical thing that needs to be changed in your own life, but rather the internal story you are telling yourself. We may not be able to change everything about the world at large, but we can change a lot about our own world. We can make decisions about what we will tolerate and what we want to experience. The choice is yours, but you must be willing to *make the change*.

CHAPTER 4

GIVE, GIVE, TAKE

There is an inescapable law of the universe: What we give is what we receive. We need to put out what we want to take in.

Want more success? Start by doing what you can to help those around you be more successful. Want more joy? Look to bring more joy to the lives of others. Want better friendships? Ask yourself what you can do to build deeper relationships.

We are united as humans by the fact that one of the best feelings we can get is the one that comes from giving. When we change someone else's day for the better, we automatically change our day for the better. Pretty simple, right?

There's a formula that I like to follow in my life, and it goes like this: **Give, give a little bit more, then take.** Or give, give, take, for short. I challenge you to give it a try and see how it works in your own life.

If you work the kind of job where you have regular meetings or go on sales calls, what would happen if the next time you went on the appointment, your mindset wasn't, "What can I get out of it for myself?" but "What can I give to someone else in the room? What can I do to make their day a little brighter or to support them in what they are working on?"

I would bet right now there is someone in your life who you know is struggling, maybe a family member who hasn't been himself lately or a co-worker or classmate who recently received bad news. What would happen if you wrote them a quick note of encouragement or reached out with a phone call or a text?

What organizations in your area are doing great work? Do they have volunteer opportunities? Monthly events where you can donate your time

WHEN WE CHANGE SOMEONE ELSE'S DAY

FOR THE BETTER,

WE AUTOMATICALLY CHANGE OUR DAY

FOR THE BETTER.

and skills? Is there room in your budget to make a financial contribution? The great thing about giving is there is absolutely no shortage of ways to do it. You do not have to be a multi-million-dollar philanthropist to give back. Time, encouragement, empathy are all valuable resources each one of us has for adding value to other people's lives.

When we place giving — not taking — first, we add value to our world. Think about that for a second. When we give, we are actually making our world *more valuable*.

If you still don't believe me, consider the science. Studies have shown that giving to others lowers blood pressure in older adults,[1] increases our satisfaction at work,[2] reduces sleep disturbances,[3] lowers the risk of depression in adolescents,[4] and helps control cortisol levels.[5] Researchers have even found that giving back stimulates the brain's reward center to release more endorphins, a phenomenon called "helper's high."[6]

The next time you catch yourself fixating on wanting *more* of something — success, happiness, inspiration — do a mental reset and ask yourself what you can do to bring *more of it* to others. The results may be better than anything you could have imagined.

[1] http://psycnet.apa.org/record/2013-21685-006

[2] https://news.wisc.edu/virtue-rewarded-helping-others-at-work-makes-people-happier/

[3] https://sleep.biomedcentral.com/articles/10.1186/s41606-017-0015-6

[4] https://news.illinois.edu/view/6367/204607

[5] https://www.sciencedirect.com/science/article/pii/S0277953618300674

[6] https://health.clevelandclinic.org/2016/11/why-giving-is-good-for-your-health/

CHAPTER 5

INVEST IN YOUR A-TEAM

Everyone has an A-Team.

Your A-Team is composed of those people in your life who you can count on to stand behind you 110 percent. It can be made up of friends or family, coworkers or neighbors. The role they play in your life isn't important; what is crucial is that they see the authentic you and provide you with unconditional support. No matter what you are going through, what obstacles you are facing, how much you have achieved or haven't, these are the people who are there for you. And you are there for them with equal commitment. That's your A-Team.

Whether we realize it or not, we all have one. Maybe your A-Team is just two people. Maybe you only interact with them once a week or a handful of times a month. Regardless, we all have an A-Team. Right now, right this very minute, you have one. None of us is ever truly alone.

That is not to say we don't experience isolation. We do. In fact, some of us struggle with feelings of isolation and loneliness on a near daily basis. But it doesn't have to be this way. By identifying our A-Team and recognizing their value in our lives and cultivating it, we can all experience more fulfillment and less isolation.

Often we get hung up focusing on the relationships that do not exist in our lives: the ideal romantic partner we want but do not have, or the superstar mentor who has yet to materialize. When we spend so much of our mental capacity ruminating over what certain relationships we *lack*, it's no wonder we end up feeling like something or someone is missing from our lives.

KNOWING THERE ARE PEOPLE IN OUR LIVES

WHO ARE TRULY THERE FOR US

WILL HELP US ACCESS PREVIOUSLY HIDDEN

RESERVES OF STRENGTH.

What would happen if instead of focusing on the people who are not in our lives, we focused on the people who are? What if instead of feeling sorry for ourselves, we practiced giving gratitude for the relationships we have?

Who is consistently there for you? Who can you count on to show up, not just when you are at your best but when you are at your worst? Who are you most genuine with? Who challenges and inspires you to do your best work? What have you done lately to show them your appreciation? What have you done to make your relationship stronger?

Generally speaking, the issue is not that we need more relationships in our lives. The issue is that we need to value the bonds we already have. We need to appreciate what these connections bring to us and practice feeling grateful for them rather than taking them for granted.

A good place to start practicing gratitude for your A-Team is by giving them actual thanks: let your friend who was there for you during your recent breakup know how much that meant to you. Say thank you to the family member who spent an hour on the phone with you going over your presentation for school or for work. Vocalizing how much you appreciate these acts of support not only strengthens your ties to your A-Team, it also recenters your focus to what you have, not what you lack.

Recognizing our A-Team and investing in our alliances builds our confidence. Knowing there are people in our lives who are truly there for us will help us access previously hidden reserves of strength. Tapping into your A-Team is like taking an amazing supplement that increases all aspects of your life. I first discovered the power of having an A-team when I was in middle school. I was not able to take conventional gym (or PE) classes, so I would go to the library instead. There I formed an incredible friendship with the school librarian. Our bond became so strong, I started eating lunch there and would share with her my struggles and successes. It was the most amazing feeling knowing that I had a teacher at my school who got me. I truly do not know how I would have made it through middle school without her compassion and understanding, plus her very honest feedback. She was not afraid to kick my butt when I needed to get into gear. Our incredible bond continues to this day, and she is truly an integral member of my A-team.

It is the people in our lives, not the things or the accolades or the commas in our bank accounts that are our biggest assets. Investing in your A-Team is simple, and it is something you can start right away. What are you waiting for?

CHAPTER 6

WHOSE LIFE ARE YOU LIVING?

Each of us has a place in this world, and that place is massive. The probability of you being born is one in four hundred trillion. Think about how many zeros that is. Pretty remarkable, right? *Our existence is intentional.* We were put here to live and fulfill our purpose.

We can only go so far living someone else's life or trying to live up to someone else's expectations for us. The question we all need to be asking ourselves is, "Whose life am I living?"

Yes, it matters what your family expects of you. It matters what your boss expects of you, or, if you are in school, what your teachers expect of you. But the number one set of expectations that matters is *your own.*

Are we staying in a relationship that is not right for us because it is the relationship our family wants us to be in? Are we feeling trapped in a job that is actually detrimental to our well-being because we think we need the title or the paycheck? Are we wasting hours projecting idealized versions of our lives onto social media without making any real and fulfilling connections?

Authenticity is a term that gets thrown around a lot these days. Like a lot of buzzwords, it can get overused and dull. But being our genuine self *does* matter. Because **the more real we are with ourselves and the world, the more we are able to achieve what we want.** Simply put, you can't achieve the life you are meant to live by being someone you aren't.

We have a choice in every single thing that we do. It is our responsibility to identify who we are and what we want, and then take action in alignment with that sense of true self.

Authenticity means stating your truth. To stand in your truth you need to identify your core values and beliefs and have a real sense of your true intentions. When you identify what matters to you, you can turn your beliefs into action. Sharing your truth with transparency and authenticity is how people get to know the real you and that is the pertinent ingredient for true human connection. Honest communication is how we find our tribe and develop a sense of community with others.

Plenty of obstacles exist that may prevent us from being our genuine selves, but the biggest is the fear of rejection. This is especially relevant to youth, but no one is immune to it. We all want to be "normal," and, paradoxically, we also want to be "unique." That balance is something every age group struggles with.

YOU CAN'T ACHIEVE THE LIFE

YOU ARE MEANT TO LIVE

BY BEING SOMEONE

YOU AREN'T.

Inauthenticity is like a drain at the bottom of a sink, sucking all of our energy, along with all of our potential. I learned this through my experience in high school. I couldn't be myself. I couldn't be the confident, big-hearted person I knew myself to be. Instead, I thought I had to be someone else. I became tough and seemingly immune to pain. Every day I was building a wall around myself just to go into the school and feel safe. If someone looked at me the wrong way, I automatically perceived it to be a personal attack, and would fight back by pouring gasoline on fire. It wasn't until I changed my environment that I realized just how taxing it was to be someone who wasn't really me, day in and day out.

The effects of inauthenticity can be very similar to the effects of depression. You steer away from the things that make you happy. You push away interests and passions that light you up. That's no way to live a life. That's no way to find fulfillment or joy.

Being real can also take on a physical aspect. I had two major leg surgeries at the age of four and eight years old. For years I was embarrassed by the noticeable scars on my legs. I thought they made me inferior and marked me as damaged. However I have come to realize that scars are the visual stories that make our lives unique and carry the potential to leave quite an impact on others. Scars do not need to be a permanent wound that we hide but rather a way for us to connect with others in a more relatable manner. Once I stopped hiding my flaws and started sharing the feelings behind them, I noticed they actually are my strengths. They remind me on a daily basis that I was able to endure the painful surgeries, the heavy casts, and the wheelchair-bound long recoveries. You too have scars and wounds that may be external or internal. When we remove the veil of shame from them, it opens us up to creating deeper connection with others.

Pretending to be someone you are not is like hanging a curtain over your face. Not only does it obscure the real version of you, but eventually that curtain is going to fall down. If you aren't being authentic, who are you trying to be? This is a question everyone should be asking themselves, because there is really no point in putting on an act.

We are born fully authentic beings. As we experience hurt and rejection, our instinct is to put up a wall of protection. But the more we resist the urge to hide behind that illusion and shatter the wall around us, the more energy we have to focus on achieving what *truly matters*.

THERE IS NO "NO"

YOU MAY ENCOUNTER MANY DEFEATS,

BUT YOU MUST NOT BE DEFEATED.

IN FACT, IT MAY BE NECESSARY TO

ENCOUNTER THE DEFEATS,

SO YOU CAN KNOW WHO YOU ARE,

WHAT YOU CAN RISE FROM,

HOW YOU CAN STILL COME OUT OF IT.

– MAYA ANGELOU

CHAPTER 7

YOU HAVEN'T FAILED YET

No matter what we have been through, no matter how painful or how stressful: we overcame it. And we will continue to overcome it. **You will not fail, because you have not failed yet.**

Maybe you didn't get that promotion — okay, there'll be another opportunity. Perhaps you lost the important game — fine, you move on to the next one. Just like success, failure is relative. You are the one who defines it and can use it as an opportunity to grow and become greater from it.

Often, when we feel like we are failing, what we need is not more success but rather a change in our perspective. The key is to not let your mistakes define your ability to move forward or paralyze you from taking action. **When we let others set our definition of success or failure, we lose out.** The things that make us feel defeated are often quite miniscule when we look at the big picture of our lives. Even when they are not, our lives are filled with resources for getting through truly difficult times — whether that is our friends, family, or our own inner will.

The view that you have of your life is not just about what the eye sees in the here and now. The perspective that we have been able to gain from all of our experiences, challenges, and adversities, as well as our incredible achievements, has built us into people who can handle just about anything. But only when we stop doubting ourselves, and letting our minds over-analyze everything. Only when we stop interpreting our adversities and setbacks as failures.

LOOK AT EVERY

OBSTACLE AS

AN INSPIRATION.

AN OPEN DOOR.

AN OPPORTUNITY.

What is failure to you? What are you letting register as failure when it really is not?

Do not let a narrow definition of success or failure be the thing that derails you from your momentum. Nothing has stopped you from getting to this point. I can assure you nothing will stop you from going further if you maintain a growth mindset, learn from mistakes, grow, and become a better person from it.

Look at every obstacle as an inspiration. An open door. An opportunity.

CHAPTER 8

GET IN THE DRIVER'S SEAT

For almost as long as I can remember, I have looked forward to learning to drive. Growing up, it never occured to me that my size might prevent me from achieving that milestone. I was simply too excited about the independence and freedom associated with driving to ever doubt that I would. But as I got older, and the time approached, the "what ifs" began to creep in: What if I could not find a car that had the features I needed? What if there wasn't a driver's ed instructor who could work with me? What if I did all that, and it still was not enough?

I was at serious risk of letting my anxiety take over, stopping me from achieving something I had wanted for so long. I knew I could not let that happen. If I wanted to *get in the driver's seat*, literally, I needed to get in the driver's seat figuratively. I needed to take action, despite my anxiety, despite my fear I might not get the outcome I had desired, perhaps a very real fear.

There is one simple action I have always been able to count on when fear of messing up is intense, and that is seeking out others who might be able to help me. So, together with my family, I started doing just that. We called the school system and spoke to the person in charge of the driver's ed program. We went to car shows where we researched just about every possible feature that I would need such as backup cameras and an electric parking brake. I contacted other little people and asked what modifications they had made to their own cars.

The more I sought out those who could help me, the more answers became clear. The more answers I found, the more my anxiety began to recede, replaced by hope.

In the end, not only was the school system completely supportive of me, but I was able to find a car that was outfitted with the features I needed. All I had to do was add pedal extenders, and I was ready to drive.

In Virginia, you can get your learner's permit when you are fifteen years and six months. On my half birthday, I applied for my permit. As of publishing, I've been a fully licensed driver for two and a half years. In the end, all of those what ifs disappeared, and as it turned out, the only thing standing in my way was a pair of metal extenders bolted onto the floor of my car coupled with some resourcefulness to get the appropriate training.

It is incredible to witness the difference between letting your anxiety take over by drawing your focus to the uncertainty versus the actual outcomes you are able to achieve when you simply commit to moving forward.

We *can* rewire the way we think. We *can* seek answers and solutions that will work for us. **Being in the driver's seat means we are not afraid**

of taking action. It means we are committed to making action our priority, even if there is a chance we will not achieve our desired outcome.

The path might not always be straight, but the answers are always out there. You just have to be willing to turn that corner and seek them out.

CHAPTER 9

WHEN ONE DOOR CLOSES FIVE MORE OPEN

Here is something I like to remind myself: all those things in my life that in the moment felt like insurmountable obstacles have turned out to be things I have been able to get past. I wouldn't be here if that weren't true, and you wouldn't be here either.

Every time we have come up against a closed door or have been standing in the doorway when it closed on us, another door has eventually opened.

GET BEHIND THE STEERING WHEEL.

PUT YOUR FOOT ON THE GAS.

SHIFT YOUR PERSPECTIVE A BIT.

Almost everyone is familiar with the phrase, *When one door closes one more opens*. My perspective on that is: **when one door closes *many more open.***

When I made the decision to finish my junior year online, I closed the door on a traditional high school experience. No homecoming, prom, parties, or friend group. Yet, in return, so many doors opened for me. Not only did I gain freedom from a destructive environment, but I had the chance to build new and meaningful relationships, advocate for a cause that will save lives, and further my ability to reach out to others through my speaking.

We limit our perspective when we think one less opportunity is going to come from a door closing. The thing about a door closing is that it usually presents an opportunity to learn. Whether it is a significant relationship coming to an end or a job that didn't work out, these experiences reveal something to us about who we are and what we want. By being open to those lessons, we come out of the experience wiser, stronger, and more resilient. And the kind of favorable circumstances that come from that? Amazing.

I love the metaphor of the doors because it lets us visualize the process by which changes come into our life. Look back on the doors that have closed in your past. How many times did that closure actually end up being a positive thing? I bet it is many. Now look forward, at all those doors up ahead just waiting for you to open.

A door closing isn't a bad thing. In fact, it's a cause for strength, hope, and optimism, if we let it be. The question is, what are you going to do? Get behind the steering wheel. Put your foot on the gas. Shift your perspective a bit. I can't wait for you to experience the results that come out of that!

CHAPTER 10

GET OUT OF YOUR OWN WAY

So many of our accomplishments hinge on this: have the mental fortitude and the courage to get out of our own way. Stop self-sabotaging and listening to the negative narratives we tell ourselves.

We are our own biggest advocates and, naturally, our own biggest critics. We often overthink our decisions, and the number one reason we do this is self protection. This way of thinking comes from our cavemen days. We needed to protect ourselves from the outside environment back then: woolly mammoths, saber-toothed tigers, and such. We are literally hardwired to react, and for good reason. Modern life has far different dangers but ones that still require vigilance.

Anxiety is the seven-letter word underneath so much of our self sabotaging. It manifests in a lot of different ways. A big one is over-analyzing — mentally going over a potential decision so much that we become paralyzed. Another is excuse-making — deciding, before we ever get started, that our efforts would be wasted. Regardless of how it presents, anxiety usually has the same outcome: it stops us from ever even taking that first step toward our goals or stops us in the process.

I know this from experience. For the first fifteen years of my life I let myself think that I didn't have anything to contribute; I didn't have much self-worth. I was trying to protect myself from being vulnerable, and during that time, I missed out on a lot.

There's a common negative feedback loop and it goes something like this: anxiety -> guilt -> self-pity -> anger. You've probably found yourself trapped in this loop before. Your anxiety stops you from doing the thing you know you need to do, you feel guilty and ashamed of your anxiety, you begin to feel sorry for yourself, and then you get angry — angry at yourself and angry at the world. But it doesn't have to be that way. Remember, you are in the driver's seat. **You have ultimate control**, and have the ability to stop anxiety from taking over.

Of course our physical experience of anxiety may not always be a choice, although great tools like breathing exercises and meditation can help us manage it. Generally speaking, our behaviors and actions are a choice. We can let anxiety win and succeed in sabotaging our best efforts, or we can get into the mindset that we are going to move forward anyway, despite whatever is in our way.

I'm not suggesting you ignore your anxiety or pretend it doesn't exist. What I am suggesting is that you stop letting it control your behaviors, stop allowing it to derail your momentum. Our anxiety is not in the driver's seat; *we are*.

Much of our anxiety — our extremely active, assertive fight or flight response — is unnecessary baggage leftover from our cavemen days. Anxiety is somewhat like our wisdom teeth: something that used to serve a purpose, but now, more often than not, just gets in our way.

I find there is power in knowing this. The more we can tell ourselves that our anxiety is normal, innate, but — for the most part — useless, the more we can change our mindset and our actions. We start recognizing the patterns that exist for us, whether it's over-thinking, excuse-making, or some other fear-driven, anxiety-fueled response. We learn to act in our best interests, even when doing so might produce uncertain outcomes. We ask for a raise or a promotion, we send that email submitting a business proposal, we find the courage to ask someone we have feelings for out on a date — not because we're free of anxiety, but because we refuse to be controlled by it and push ourselves to move past it.

Here's the truth: We all have a tremendous toolkit of talents and resources inside of us right now, just waiting to be used. When we get out of our own way, when we stop allowing fear and uncertainty to control our decision-making, we finally start to move toward all those amazing things that are right over the finish line.

And that is so worth it.

CHAPTER 11

LEARN TO SIT WITH DISCOMFORT

We need to learn to sit with discomfort, to get a little comfortable with things that aren't comfortable. The places of hardships we experience present the greatest opportunities for learning and growth.

Discomfort can take a lot of forms: Sometimes it feels like anxiety, hurt or conflict. It usually appears in those areas of our lives where we know there is something that we need to do, but we are avoiding it due to the difficult or unpleasant reactions we think will occur.

If there is someone in our life with whom we need to make amends, it can be uncomfortable to say the words "I'm sorry." If we have romantic feelings for someone, it can feel really difficult to find a way to tell them. If we want to be considered for a particular promotion at work, it can be tremendously scary to make that known. I get that; it is extremely hard to face those feelings.

But here's the thing: There is no way around it. We can't get the positive results we are seeking if we're not willing to experience those difficult feelings. Period.

In fact, I would go as far as to say that how we deal with discomfort plays a vital role in whether we move forward in life or stay stuck where we are. Almost every leap forward in our lives — whether personal, professional, or otherwise requires some amount of anguish.

Are you letting your fear of discomfort hold you back in life? Are there things you need to be doing but aren't because of the difficult feelings that you're afraid will come from it?

You don't need to beat yourself up for feeling this way. As humans, we all experience anxiety and discomfort and look for ways to avoid it — that's a given. But it is our job to get past it. Because feeling uncomfortable really is small in comparison to the rewards that are waiting for us on the other side.

Often getting to the root of why we're experiencing fear can go a long way to helping us push through it. Frequently, what we're seeking to prevent by avoiding uncomfortable situations is being rejected or told no. We're afraid our apology won't be accepted. That our romantic interest won't reciprocate our feelings. That we'll be turned down for the promotion. The funny thing is, those are the exact results we are *guaranteed* when we avoid taking the risk in the first place.

Because, really, what's the worst possible outcome? You hear "no"? Then you are just in the same place where you started. Actually, you're not in that same place because you've been able to show yourself that the door is always right there. Are you choosing to walk through it? Or are you letting your anxiety and fear hold you back?

Say the words, have the conversation, make your wishes known. Learn to take steps despite the uncertainty that comes with them. Whatever the outcome, when you get past discomfort, you win.

CHAPTER 12

NO NEED TO HIDE YOUR SCARS

Behind every experience of pain there is potential for purpose. Whatever the cause of our suffering, however difficult or impossible it feels to us in the moment, there is always an opportunity to do or make something great from it.

When I left the toxic environment of my high school behind, two big things happened. The first was that I was able to use the new free time and flexibility in my schedule to accelerate my purpose of sharing my story with others and motivating them to be their biggest success. The second was that I testified in front of the Virginia

General Assembly to help advocate for new anti-bullying legislation.

About a month after I began online school, my family and I sat down and had a conversation. We knew that I wasn't alone in suffering abuse and bullying from other students. We knew there were tens of thousands of youth from all over the state, and across the country going through what I had, many of whom likely didn't have the resources I did to have the dialogue and find solutions. It was great that I had been able to positively impact my situation and remove myself from that environment. But what about the kids who were still stuck? Together as a family, we decided that we would do something to tackle the problem.

We became resourceful and reached out to our good family friend who is a Virginia state delegate. I shared my story with her, and based on my experience, she drafted a bill that requires administrators to convey the results of a bullying investigation to parents of both the victim and the perpetrator within five days of the incident.

LET THE PAIN

BE YOUR FUEL.

LET IT BE THE THING

THAT PROPELS YOU FURTHER

THAN YOU EVER THOUGHT

YOU COULD GO.

It's not something that will change lives instantly. But it is another mechanism in place to proactively communicate with families dealing with bullying, making their hardship a little less stressful.

The bill went to the House Education Subcommittee and made its way through the House and the Senate. Our initial meeting occurred at the end of January 2017, and by June, the then-governor of Virginia, Terry McAuliffe, signed the bill into law.

My family and I joined Governor McAuliffe the day he signed the bill. Also there were two families who had lost their teenagers to suicide as a result of severe cyberbullying.

The dire consequences of bullying are no secret. Even still, I was surprised how deeply impactful it was to interact with those families. It is one thing to think about bullying in the abstract; it is another to see the faces of parents and siblings who have lost someone dear. My hope is, of course, that there will be fewer grieving families, fewer lives ending too soon, because of the bill that promotes more proactive communication.

The bottom line is, *we all suffer*. We all face trauma and tragedies in life. What makes the difference in our outcomes isn't whether or not we hurt, but what we do with that pain. What action we take with it.

Suffering is an easy place to get trapped. It is more automatic for most of us to keep our focus directed toward the people and things that are the source of our pain instead of looking outward to see what we can do, how we can grow or turn our pain into something meaningful. I know that, because I've done it. In the past, I let myself get stuck in feelings of self-pity or wanting revenge. It is okay if we feel that way from time to time. We are human, after all. But we must not stay there as it prevents us from moving forward.

Getting trapped in a negative mindset means getting trapped in our pain. Ironically, we only suffer more when we do that. We begin to suffer not just from the pain itself, but from our inability to move on. And, really, what is the point of letting ourselves do that? What is the point of allowing negativity — allowing things we never asked for or wanted in our lives — to end up being the things that direct us, or, more often, leave us directionless?

I get it: this is hard. You can't snap your fingers and say "pain go away" or "trauma go away." But you can take it somewhere.

Let the pain be your fuel. Let it be the thing that propels you further than you ever thought you could go.

CREATING YOUR BIGGEST SUCCESS

THE NEXT TIME YOU SEE SOMEONE

THAT YOU THINK IS SUCCESSFUL,

DON'T FOCUS ON WHAT THEY'RE

DOING NOW. FOCUS ON WHAT

THEY DID TO GET THERE.

– JAY SHETTY

CHAPTER 13

HAVE A "MAKE THINGS HAPPEN" MINDSET

By now, the story is famous: A single mother living with the assistance of welfare gets the idea for a children's book and spends her free time writing a manuscript. When it's done, she sends it to publishers and is promptly rejected not by one, not by two, but by twelve different publishing houses. Finally it is picked up by Bloomsbury, but even they are lukewarm about it, encouraging the author to "keep her day job." The book, *Harry Potter and the Sorcerer's Stone*, launches the most popular book series of all times, selling more than 450 million copies worldwide and making its author, J.K. Rowling, the first writer to become a billionaire.

There are dozens of examples just like this: Lady Gaga got dropped from her record label after just three months. Stephen King's first novel, *Carrie*, was declined by 30 publishers. Steven Spielberg was rejected from University of Southern California School of Cinematic Arts not once, but twice. As a child, Thomas Edison was told by a teacher he was "too stupid to learn anything." He was also fired from his first two jobs. Henry Ford's first two attempts to start automobile companies ended in bankruptcies.

What all of these individuals have in common, despite their odds-defying success, is that they might have just as easily given up. Each one of them encountered a roadblock that they could have used as an opportunity to say "I've had enough." And likely, no one would have faulted them. After all, they tried.

What a loss that would have been, not just for them but for the world.

We will all hit dead ends in our lives. We will all hear the word "no." That is inevitable. The question we need to be asking ourselves when that happens is not "Why?" but "What's next?" "Where do I go from here?" The next thing we try may result in a "no" too. That's okay. It doesn't mean we've failed.

Many of us settle in our lives for a see-what-happens attitude. But what we really need is a make-things-happen mindset. The key word there is *make*. It's action. Knowing what we want is great, but it's not going to come together without action, without us doing something about it. What point is there in realizing how we want our lives to change if we don't go out there and change them?

We need to bring our actions in line with our mindsets. Making things happen means you are committed to taking initiative to advance what you want. It means when you do experience those inevitable setbacks, you choose not to take them personally or use them as excuses to give up. You're ready with the next plan of attack and the one after that. It took J.K. Rowling thirteen attempts to find a publisher. What if she had stopped after the second or third or even twelfth attempt?

We simply cannot afford to live a life of "what ifs." Too much is at stake: our progress, our purpose, our fulfillment.

The good news is that the more often we take initiative, the easier it gets. We gain a little more mastery over our anxiety, feel a little less sting when that rejection or setback occurs. We become smarter and savvier. Taking the next step becomes our habit or default, not the thing we have to talk ourselves into.

We are the ones responsible for creating our greatest success. The things we hope to achieve, the things we know we're capable of — they can and will be ours. We can truly do and become whatever our minds think of. But only if we match imagination with action. **Only if we commit to going forward no matter what.**

CHAPTER 14

BE YOUR OWN HERO

The simplest definition of a hero is this: a person we admire because they do something or possess some skill that we aspire to, that is somehow greater than or beyond our own.

But what if we could take that skill on for ourselves? **What if whatever characteristic we looked up to in that other person was something we were able to adopt for ourselves, even in the smallest of ways?** We would, quite literally, start to become our own heroes.

What traits, behaviors, and skill sets do our heroes possess that would serve us if we took them on?

What is in their toolkit that we could benefit from by adding to ours? We may not become like that person overnight — and that shouldn't be our goal anyway. But when we learn from our heroes, we bring ourselves that little extra something that adds to our greatness.

A straightforward example of this is one of the most common types of heros for kids and young people: athletes. Most of us probably aren't going to achieve the batting average of Derek Jeter or the playmaking skills of LeBron James. But if you take on even a fraction of Jeter or LeBron's commitment to training and practice, your game is guaranteed to improve.

Being our own hero means we are not content to just admire our heros. It means we are actively seeking to understand what it is we admire about them and looking to apply at least some sliver of that to our own lives.

When I say understanding what we admire about that person, I don't mean the flashy, superficial things like money, power, or influence. I'm talking about the deeper qualities, the underlying character traits that made their success possible. For athletes, that might mean commitment to training. For an artist, it could mean their willingness to take creative risks. Figure out what it is, and start putting it into practice.

In my own life, my biggest hero is Tony Robbins. There's a lot to admire about Tony, but the number-one thing I'm in awe of is the sheer energy and dedication he puts into leaving a legacy of an improved world. Every day, I try to take a little of that on for myself. And here's the cool thing: Even if I only achieve five percent of what Tony has, I know the impact I make on the world will still be huge.

CHAPTER 15

MANIFEST WHAT YOU WANT

In April of 2017 I was speaking at a business networking group just outside of Richmond. After my talk, an audience member asked an interesting question: "Who is your biggest hero?"

I didn't have to think about that one.

"Tony Robbins," I told her. "I'd love to meet him one day."

Afterwards, another attendee came over to introduce herself to me. Her name was Christina and a few minutes into our conversation she shared that she grew up in Texas and that she had worked with one of Tony's business partners.

"I would love to see what I can do to connect you two," she told me.

My first thought was, *Yeah right. You're going to connect me with Tony freaking Robbins?*

But I smiled and said thank you, and we exchanged contact information.

Two weeks later I got a call while I was in Denver. It was Christina.

"I just got off the phone with Tony's executive assistant," she said. "Tony has heard about you and has invited you as his personal guest to his next event."

A few months later I traveled with my mom and Christina to Newark, New Jersey, for Tony's *Unleash the Power Within* (UPW), a four-day event that turned out to be Tony's largest live event to date —14,000 people.

The first day, we sat in the invitational VIP section on the wings of the stage, only a few feet away from Tony. While there, I met the head of live events for Tony, a man named Jason. We struck up a conversation and hit it off. At the start of the second day, I approached Jason and asked, "So when am I going to get to meet Tony?" Note, I didn't ask "Can I meet Tony?" I didn't say "Would I be able to?" I said "When can I?" I knew this opportunity was too good, too rare, not to make a move.

And it ended up happening.

At the end of the first day of UPW Tony stages a signature experience: walking on fire. We stood in a parking lot outside the arena. A bonfire had been going all day; "production assistants" scooped the coals into dozens of lanes (remember, it had to hold 14,000 people.) Those of us in the invitational section would be in Tony's lane.

When the time came for Tony's turn, I walked up to his lane and went with him. He held my hand as I walked over the thousand-degree coals.

The last night of the program lasted until 2:00 in the morning. As we were getting ready to leave, Jason came up to me and told me he would bring me backstage. It was nearly 2:30 a.m. when I finally met Tony.

For a few minutes, I racked my brain, trying to plan out what I was going to say. I wanted to articulate the perfect sentences. But I realized that wasn't what I should be doing. Instead I realized I have to be in the moment, that's what he would expect, or as he terms it, "playing full out".

I said to him, "Tony, I know you get this all day, but you have given me more than anyone else. Thank you." Then I said, "You know, I've been told I'm the next version of you."

He looked at me and smiled. "Oh good, we're twins," he said.

It was just a brief encounter. Afterward, Tony left and I went back to my hotel room. But it was the start of so much more.

I didn't know it at the time, but what I did that weekend in Newark was manifest what I wanted to make happen. I knew it was my dream to meet

Tony Robbins, and I knew that I had been given an amazing opportunity to do so.

It is so powerful the way manifestation works. When you tell your brain, "It's going to happen," you seek out how to make it happen — you seek out the people and situations that are going to make it happen. You realize how the universe puts the right people and situations in your path.

Going to Newark, I knew I had to make meeting Tony happen. I didn't know how or under what exact circumstances I would do so. But I knew this opportunity was too good to let slip by.

I told myself that it was going to happen, and that an opportunity would present itself, when the time was right, for me to make it happen. And it did.

Remember, *the universe is out for your success.* When we are on the path we are meant to be on, things start to happen. We need to be ready to seize upon them when they do. To not ask if, but when.

CHAPTER 16

SURROUND YOURSELF WITH WHO YOU WANT TO BECOME

One of the most surefire ways we can manifest what we want in our lives is to surround ourselves with the right people.

That doesn't mean you have to surround yourself with a bunch of C-Suite executives of Fortune 50 companies. It doesn't have to be about a title. But you should surround yourself with people you aspire to be like in some way, people that add to your life.

Maybe that means people who make full use of their sense of humor, or their energy, or empathy. Whatever it is, focus on those people. And learn from the way they live their lives and see what you can adopt to your own journey.

Ideally, social connections would all be driven by a desire to surround ourselves with people who will support and uplift us, either in action or by example. But, of course, we all know that is often not the case. Sometimes fear of being alone compels us to settle for relationships that do not serve us. This is especially true in romantic relationships, but it can be true in our friendships, our working relationships, and even our familial relationships.

When we have a clear understanding of what we want, what we value, in ourselves and our interactions — whether it's a friendship, a romantic relationship, a working partnership — we can then seek it out. We're aware of what we want to see and have around us, and we're more likely to have it in our lives. Until we learn to identify the qualities we want and value, we are not able to recognize them in others. We let the wrong people into our lives, while letting the right ones slip away like water through our fingers.

I'm not saying you have to go around with a bulleted list of character traits in your pocket that you consult every time you meet someone new. We can live in the moment, follow our intuition. We can experiment. But the greater attention we pay to specific traits, the more practice we give to recognizing them, the better our intuition will be, the more we'll be able to surround ourselves with the kind of people who truly add value to our lives. What we focus on is what we see.

The thing is, relationships are a huge driving force in our lives. And that is true whether we are taking the time to think about what we want to get from them or whether we aren't. Think about that. This is a huge area of our lives — personal, familial, romantic, professional — and some of us are putting more thought into what we want to order for lunch.

Here's something I've learned through my experiences: most successful people want to help others achieve success. You wouldn't believe the people I have connected with just over the last couple of years. People who are at the top of their fields. People who are absolute titans and have mastered their craft. People who you might think wouldn't have time to give to someone less prominent than themselves. But they often generously give the time. You could say "So-and-so doesn't have time for me" or "She would never return my email." Or you could ask yourself, "What might happen if I tried?"

Not all "mentors" have to be people we have face-to-face relationships with. If your dream mentor is Bill Gates, I'm not suggesting you fly to Medina and scale his gates to ask him to get coffee with you. But you can read interviews about him, listen to a podcast he is featured in or watch YouTube videos. You don't necessarily have to cultivate a close, in-person relationship with someone to bring them into your life. Technology is a great tool to make this happen, and there is no reason why we cannot constantly learn from remarkable leaders.

When we surround ourselves with the right people, we surround ourselves with inspiration. The more we can be around those people and around that energy, the better people we will be.

You don't get what you don't ask for.

CHAPTER 17

FULFILLMENT= SUCCESS

When I go out and give talks, I meet people of every age and background. I encounter brand-new high schoolers, and I get to know C-suite executives decades into their careers. Because of this cross section of experiences, I often hear from people who claim they haven't achieved any great successes in their lives yet. They haven't done that one thing that others would look at and call remarkable. That feeling is understandable, but my counter to it is always the same: Are you fulfilled? That is my ultimate definition of success: fulfillment.

Have you ever noticed how sometimes the people with the most — the most resources, the most money, the most "success"— are also the most miserable? And sometimes it's the people with the least who are the happiest, the most seemingly fulfilled?

We could look at a social media account with 70,000 followers and call that a success. But that person could have no achievements, no accolades, no substance. We could look at someone with a bank account with multiple commas in it and call that a success, too. But that individual could be absolutely miserable, dreading waking up in the morning and going into work.

Fulfillment is different. Fulfillment is less about what is observable from the outside, and more about how we feel and what we know about ourselves from the inside. Fulfillment is a sense of contentment, peace, and gratitude about our life. It is the knowledge that we are on our correct paths and we are contributing to the world in the way we are uniquely meant to. Fulfillment is a feeling of satisfaction and happiness. I make the effort to reinforce this on a daily basis as I strive to connect and positively impact those I come in contact with. It is a muscle that I work out as often as I can.

Intuition is a powerful driver on the road to fulfillment. I believe we know instinctively when we are not on the paths we are meant to be on, when we are not setting ourselves up for this feeling of happiness. But we often ignore the warning signs in our own body — our sluggishness, our depression, our lack of enthusiasm for getting out of bed in the morning and greeting the day. We ignore these signs, we push by them as if we have blinders on. Why? Fear we won't be able to have or do any better. Fear we *aren't* any better. And our over-reliance on superficial definitions of success that leave us feeling drained and purposeless.

We all know what fulfillment looks like because we see the fulfilled people around us. They are immediately recognizable. They are the people who radiate contentment, the people who, regardless of the stressors of their lives and their work, seem to never lack energy or enthusiasm.

Maybe you've never really considered the origins of the word fulfillment. The meaning is right there in the word itself: to be filled, to make full. Fulfilled people seem to have more energy because they are actually being *filled* each time they go out into the world and live their purpose.

The great thing about fulfillment is that it's self-perpetuating. The more fulfillment we get, the more we seek. One small action, one tiny shift toward more fulfillment, can set the ball rolling and lead to the next action and the one after that. **Remember, momentum is a powerful force.**

When I altered my high school environment and I began down my path of completing my education while speaking with and motivating others, the reversal in my outlook and contentment was immediate. And it has only gotten better as I meet more people, touch more lives, step further into my purpose. Has it always been perfect? No. Has the journey been 100 percent free of obstacles and setbacks? Of course not. But every time I hear feedback that my message has helped someone shift their perspective or get closer to their goals,

WE CAN BUILD LIVES

WHERE WE STRIVE FOR MORE

THAN MERELY SUPERFICIAL SUCCESS,

BUT RATHER TRUE FULFILLMENT.

it reaffirms for me that I am doing what I am meant to be doing. It helps provide me with the energy and drive to keep going no matter what.

And we need to keep going, no matter what. We need to keep our momentum pointed in the direction of positive outcomes.

One of the great things about fulfillment in contrast to other definitions of success is that fulfillment is ours to keep regardless of the specifics of what we're going through in a given moment. When we are on a mission that is marked with personal contentment, we can experience stressors and setbacks without being knocked off course. Because we know they are a temporary and inevitable part of life. Those disruptions and obstacles that used to feel insurmountable are now shrunk down into their real size. It doesn't matter if you are one day or three decades into your journey, you can experience life's valleys and still be fulfilled if you know you are finally on the right track.

Over the course of a single year, I went from someone who dreaded getting up in the morning, someone whose relationships with friends and family were reaching a breaking point, to someone who starts each day with a sense of excitement and motivation and who has more fulfilling relationships than I ever imagined possible. And here's the thing: I don't think I'm remarkable in that regard. I don't think I'm the exception. I think you can have this shift in your life, too. It starts by challenging the way you think and then putting your new way of thinking into action.

We need to set our own definitions of success, and we need to be thoughtful and purposeful in the definitions we choose. We can and will build lives based on purpose and genuine contentment. We can build lives where we strive for more than merely superficial success, but rather true fulfillment.

So what gives you a sense of purpose? What fills you with energy and drive, even when things get tough? What makes you feel like you're not just getting by in the world, but making it a better place? That's step one.

Now that you know these answers, step two is determining what actions you are going to take. Just thinking about it isn't enough, we need to take action. That's how we get results. That's how we live the life we were meant to live.

CLOSING

Let's be honest, things are absolutely terrible sometimes. We get into nasty fights, lose a loved one, get laid off, face rejection. But the gift of living with intention, passion, and purpose is what can convert the adversity we face into transformative growth.

For years, I hated being in my own skin. I was ashamed and humiliated and didn't feel as if my life had any meaning to it. I used to view my rare skeletal condition as a barrier to feeling joy. The world changed for me when I decided to change the lens through which I see life as a whole and shift my focus to being grateful for all I do have rather than feeling inadequate for what I lack. You have tremendous gifts inside of you.

Be the inspiration for someone to be their best self by starting with yourself and being of service to others. The more you give, the more you get. Time is our most precious resource, and we do not need a diagnosis or a tragic event to remind us of this.

I hope I have shifted your perspective a bit and encouraged you to live your life with curiosity by seeking out new possibilities. Remember to live outside your comfort zone, as that creates incredible opportunities. How we see the world determines the world that we live in. Look up, live big and innovate your own solution by turning obstacles into opportunities for growth, transformation and fulfillment.

Made in the USA
Columbia, SC
10 November 2018